Manufactured by Amazon.ca
Bolton, ON

10661971R00061